BookLife
freedom
Readers
T0016344
LIVES
OF
BUTTERFLIES
BY HOLLY DUHIG

BookLife PUBLISHING

BookLife Publishing Ltd.
King's Lynn
Norfolk PE30 4LS

ISBN: 978-1-80155-143-4

Printed in Poland.

Written by:
Holly Duhig

Edited by:
Charlie Ogden

Designed by:
Danielle Webster-Jones

A catalogue record for this book is available from the British Library

BookLife freedom Readers

Photo Credits

Cover & throughout – Boule, Super Prin, suns07butterfly, Le Do, Eric Isselee, jps, Jausa, mashe, oksana2010, Ian 2010, Feng Yu, Tischenko Irina, Elena Elisseeva, Denise Torres, sakhorn. 2 – grafvision,4 – Sari ONeal. 5 – Super Prin. 6 – Zdenek Kubik. 7 – KULISH VIKTORIIA. 8 – Rosalba Matta Machado. 9 – Anest. 10 – THEJAB. 11 – Mathisa. 12 – Beata Becla. 13 – Grapevine. 14 – Victoria M Gardner. 15 – Protasov AN. 16 – Anettphoto. 17 – Jakub Zak. 18 – IVP. 19 – majeczka. Images are courtesy of Shutterstock.com. With thanks to Getty Images, Thinkstock Photo and iStockphoto. 20main – Sharon Day 20b – studio on line. 21 – Pan Xunbin. 22 – Mayura Ladaeng, Boule, Matee Nuserm, Ken Tannenbaum, Valentyna Chukhlyebova.

CONTENTS

WHAT IS A BUTTERFLY?

Butterflies are insects with six legs and two antennae. They are known for having bright and colourful wings.

A butterfly is a living thing. It needs food and water to live. Its wings help it fly around and find food. Butterflies use their antennae to smell. They are like two very long noses.

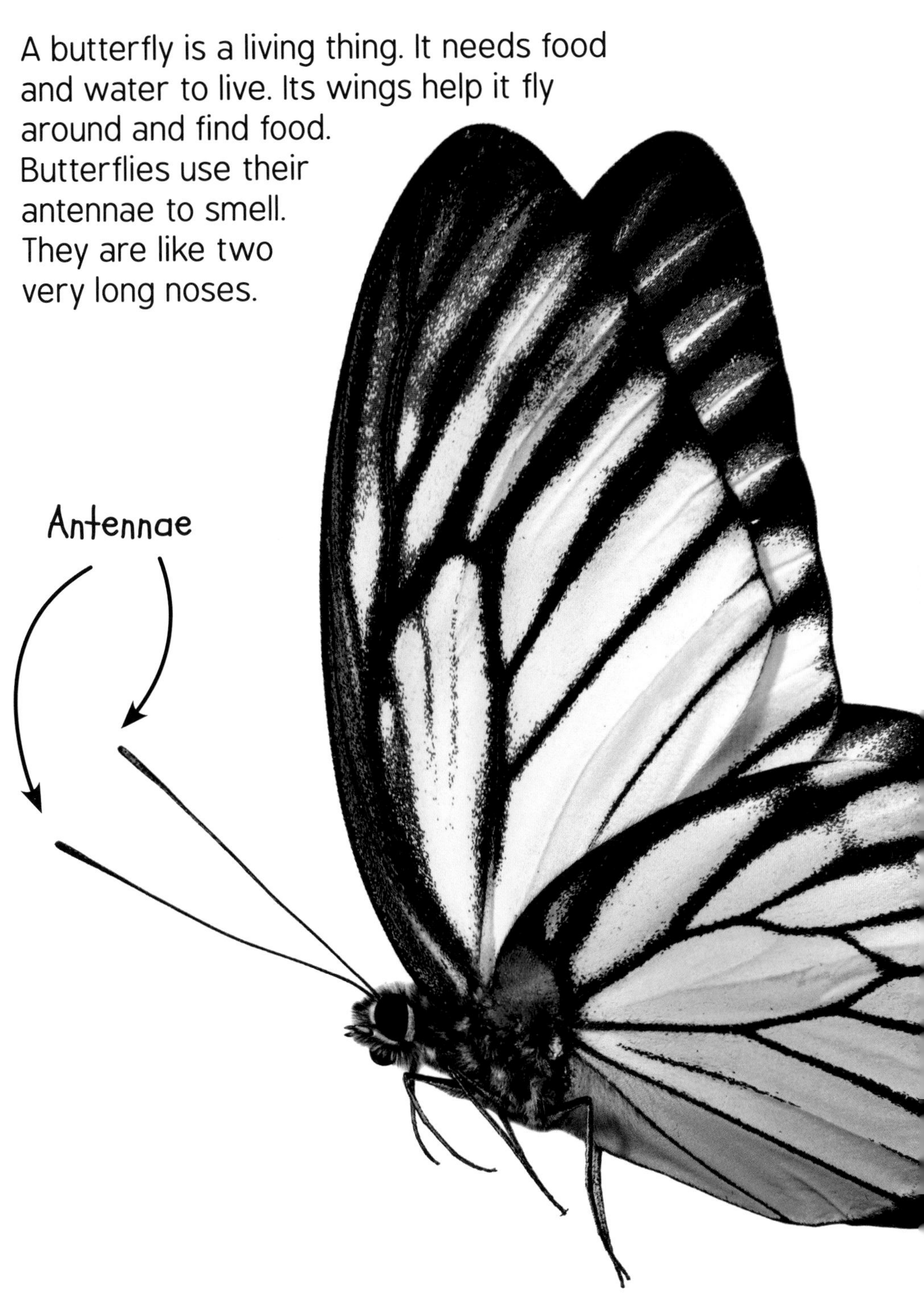

WHAT DOES A BUTTERFLY LOOK LIKE?

A butterfly has four wings. Different butterflies have different patterns on their wings. This is a peacock butterfly. Its wings are red with four spots.

The bodies of butterflies are very long and thin. They have long legs, which they can use to taste leaves. This is how they decide which leaf to lay their eggs on.

HOW DO BUTTERFLIES LAY EGGS?

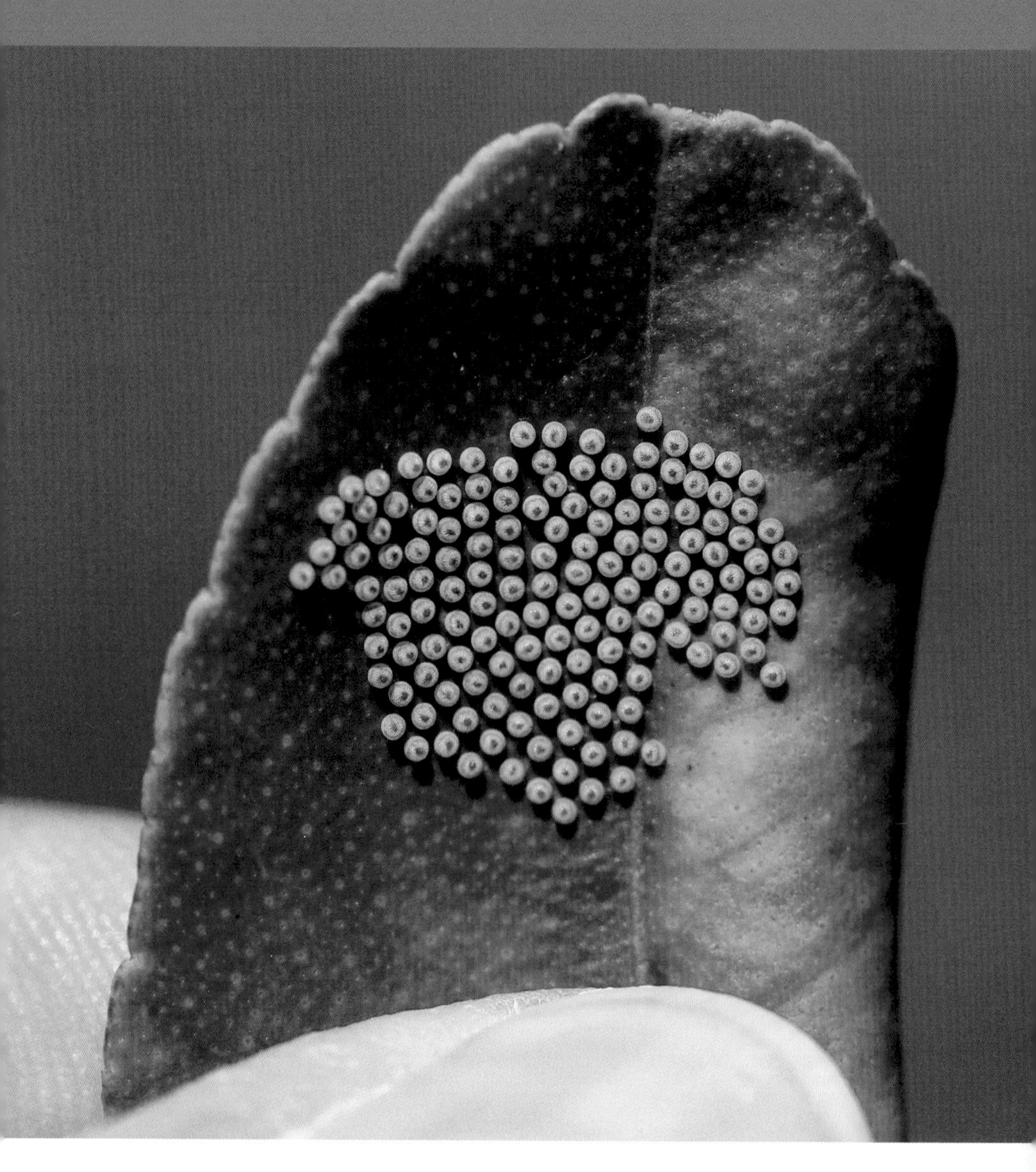

Female butterflies lay their eggs on the underside of leaves. This protects the eggs from the rain. The eggs do not fall off because they are very sticky.

A caterpillar hatches from each egg. A caterpillar begins life by eating the leaf that it hatched on.

CURLY CATERPILLARS

Caterpillars have long bodies without wings, and they spend most of their time eating leaves. When caterpillars have eaten enough leaves, they make themselves a chrysalis.

A chrysalis is a hard shell that keeps the caterpillar safe while it changes into a butterfly. It stays in its chrysalis for about two weeks before emerging.

WHERE DO BUTTERFLIES LIVE?

Butterflies live outdoors where there are lots of plants and flowers. They like to live in places with warm weather.

When it rains, butterflies use trees and rocks to protect themselves. You can help butterflies by putting a butterfly house in your garden for them to use when it rains.

WHAT DO BUTTERFLIES EAT?

Butterflies have a long straw-like tongue called a proboscis. Butterflies use their proboscis to drink the nectar in flowers.

Butterflies often drink from puddles because they are not very deep. They also eat fruit when they can find it.

WHAT DO BUTTERFLIES DO?

Butterflies usually only live for two to four weeks. Most of this time is spent trying to find a mate so they can lay eggs.

Butterflies have eyes that are very good at spotting bright colours, such as the colours on another butterfly's wings. This makes it easier for them to find a mate. Butterflies are also good at spotting the bright colours of flowers. This helps them find food.

HOW DO BUTTERFLIES HELP?

Butterflies help new flowers to grow. When butterflies drink nectar, they collect pollen from the flower on their legs.

Butterflies carry this pollen to the next flower they land on. This flower then uses the pollen to make seeds. These seeds then grow into new flowers.

BEAUTIFUL BUTTERFLIES

The monarch butterfly lives in North America. It has a ten centimetre wingspan, which is the distance between the tips of its wings.

The dead-leaf butterfly looks like an autumn leaf.
This makes it harder for other animals to spot it.

FUN FACTS

Instead of using their tongues, butterflies taste things with their feet. Female butterflies usually live for longer and are bigger than male butterflies.

The largest butterfly in the world is the Queen Alexandra's birdwing. This butterfly's wingspan can be over 25 centimetres.

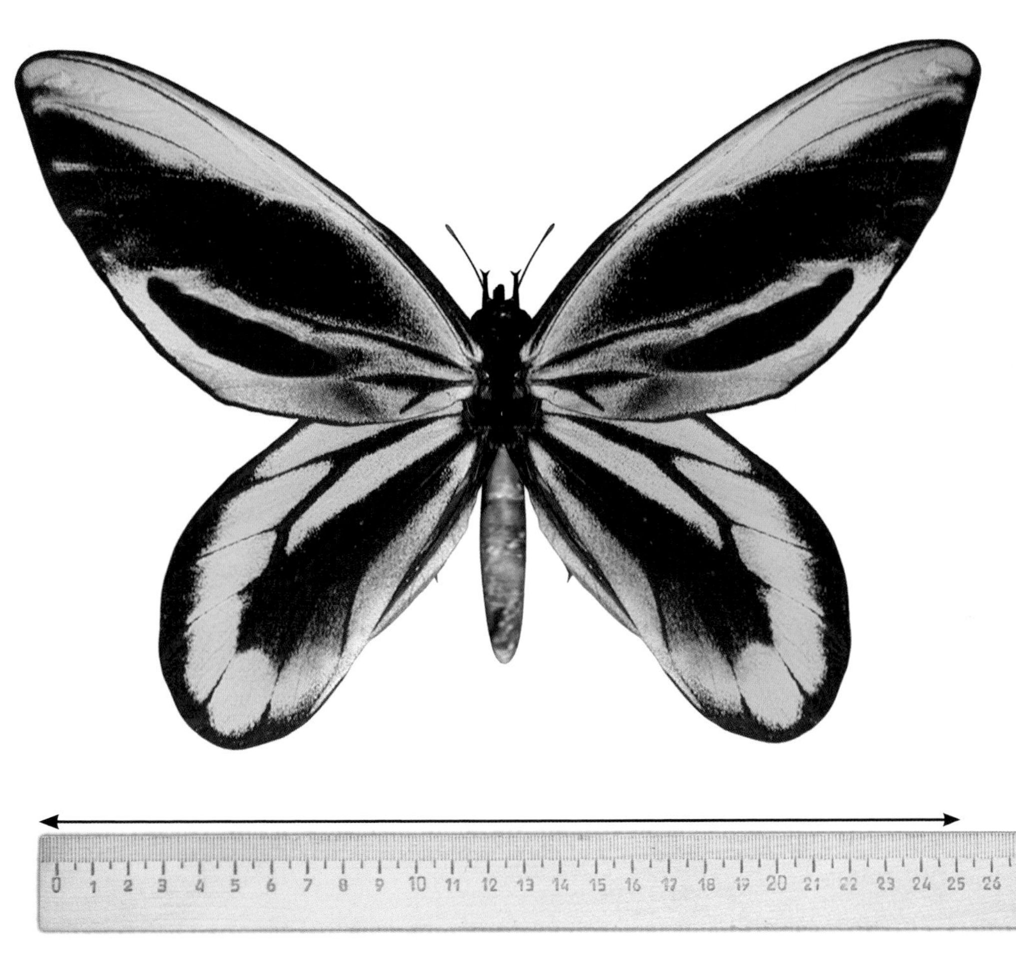

QUESTIONS

1: How many legs do butterflies have?

2: Where do butterflies lay their eggs?

3: What is a butterfly's tongue called?
a) Antennae
b) Feeler
c) Proboscis

4: How do butterflies help new flowers to grow?

5: Which is your favourite butterfly? What do you like about it?